Learning to Listen
with Significant Others

A Conversational Approach

Bob Bohlken, Ph.D.
Emeritus Professor of Communication

All inquiries should be addressed to:
Images Unlimited Publishing
P.O. Box 305
Maryville, MO 64468
660-582-4605

info@imagesunlimitedpublishing.com
http://www.imagesunlimitedpublishing.com

ATTN: Quantity discounts are available to your educational institution, organization, corporation or industry for reselling, educational purposes, subscription incentives, gifts, or fund-raising campaigns.

First Edition
ISBN 978-0-930643-23-2
Printed in the United States of America.
Interior drawings by Carol Farrens.
Cover and interior page design by Teresa Carter.

Table of Contents

Learning to Listen with Significant Others 1
    Purpose for Interpersonal Verbal Communication
    Listening Behavior Questionnaire

Listening – A Language Skill 5
    Listening Defined
    Communication Climate

Types/Purposes for Listening 11
    Discriminative Listening
    Comprehensive Listening
    Critical Listening
    Statement of Fact, Inference and Implied/Opinion
    Comparison
    Closing Process
    Relationship/Empathetic Listening

**Physical Context and Time Influences
on Listening Effectiveness** 59
    Time Consideration
    Levels
    Axis
    Space/Proximity/Furniture

DEDICATION

This book is dedicated to the founders and members of the International Listening Association (ILA).

I attribute my motivation to study and promote the skill of listening to my membership in ILA. Much of the material, including the jokes, in this book are based on my experiences and presentations at ILA conferences.

I became a member of ILA in 1984 with the encouragement of Manny and Dee Steil, whom I had not met. Manny founded the organization in 1979 in honor of Ralph Nichols, University of Minnesota Communication Professor Emeritus, who initiated the formal study of listening as a language skill.

In 1984 I relinquished my responsibilities as the head of the Division of Communication at Northwest Missouri State University, Maryville, Missouri, in order to devote time to the teaching and development of courses in listening and semantics, both areas of special interest to me. At the 1984 ILA Conference I became involved in the Committee on Education and promoted the development of listening competency standards for secondary schools and *Swap Shops for Listening Teaching Methods*. Since then I have served two terms on the ILA Board of Directors (one of which I was vice president). I am a life member and have presented papers at all but four conferences. I was recognized with the Special Recognition Award in 1999 and was inducted into International Listening Association's Hall of Fame in 2006. Of all the professional organizations with which I have been affiliated, ILA members are the greatest.

Because of ILA, I was able to establish at Northwest Missouri State University a culture of listening before I retired in 2000 after serving the institution for 30 years. The basic listening course was a requirement in the communication major; it was an elective in the general studies, in the business management program, and in the secondary teachers' education program. A session on classroom lecture listening was a part of the freshman seminar program. During my tenure at Northwest, I had four independent study students present classroom listening research papers at ILA conferences.

Since my retirement, I continue to promote the culture of listening, the objective of this book. "Mother Mary," my one and only spouse for 55 years, and I developed the interpersonal communication unit with emphasis on listening for St. Gregory's Catholic Church's *Marriage Preparation Course*. I stress the importance of listening in my local newspaper column and in my leisure reading children's books and story-telling books. I continue to give local programs in the community and at the area high school on interpersonal listening behaviors. Thanks to ILA!

PREFACE

As with all interpersonal communication, there needs to be a mutual purpose on the parts of the communicators. The purpose for this book is to provide you with the means by which you and your significant other(s) can improve your interpersonal verbal or language listening skills. The book is written in an informal, conversational style intended to be shared simultaneously with one or several others exchanging roles of reader(s) and listener(s).

I have studied and taught the English language skills (reading, writing, listening and speaking) for close to 50 years. The contents of this book are a capsule of the principles of face-to-face listening that I have gleaned from my research and experiences. My credibility is based on Aristotle's ethos principles: 1) knowledge/wisdom, 2) moral standards and 3) goodwill or caring about your learning to improve yourself. I am a teacher who gains satisfaction from helping others learn.

You must decide my credibility when reading this material because I am not attributing much of the information to other sources. That is why I chose to use *conversational* (based on 50 years of research and teaching) rather than *academic* presentational style. Specific attribution of material is academically sound but distracts from the messages' content and interest.

In order for this book to be effective, you and your significant other(s) must realize the importance that effective listening has in both your interpersonal and public communication. You must be willing to devote the time and mutual efforts to help one another improve his/her listening to language skills. I can only provide the means, but only you together can make the experiences successful.

I suggest that you share one book; each alternating the roles of reading aloud and listening to the information provided. After each arbitrary segment of reading and listening, you should discuss the material for mutual comprehension. There are experiences/activities dispersed throughout the book that are essential for your understanding and practice of effective listening skills.

Before you delve into this interpersonal listening study, consider your intrapersonal communication listening. The following poem has had wide-spread publication and international attention.

Listen to the One in the Mirror
by Bob Bohlken

When life's choices come your way,
Listen to what others have to say.
But when all is said and done,
Look into a mirror and listen to the reflected one.

When temptations are laid at your door,
And promises are yours to take,
Discuss the consequences and more,
But listen to the one in the mirror for your own sake.

You may fool the world throughout the years,
Others may admire you as you pass.
But you'll suffer heartache and tears,
If you don't listen to the one in the glass.

It is you alone who makes your choices,
No matter what others may say or do.
You may listen to other voices,
But the voice of the one in the mirror is true.

Learning to Listen with Significant Others

"Please listen to me!"

"Please pay attention to what I have to say!"

"Please give me your undivided attention!"

Do you ever want to use these expressions in regard to others in an interpersonal, face-to-face, spoken communication? Do you think others want to use these expressions in regard to you in interpersonal face-to-face and public spoken communication situations?

The following poem brings out some of the problems, hopes, and desires encountered in interpersonal communication. See whether any of these situations sound familiar in your life.

Please Listen to Me
by Bob Bohlken

When I want you to listen to me, you immediately give me all kinds of advice;
When I want you to listen to me, you tell me I shouldn't feel the way I do.
When I want you to listen to me, you try to solve my problems before we hear
   them through.
You are not really listening; you are talking and thinking you are being nice.

When I want you to listen to me, you treat me as if I'm helpless and dumb.
When I want you to listen to me, you try to convince me that my fears are
   unfounded and untrue.
When I want you to listen to me, you tell me my feelings are irrational to you.
You really are not listening; you are telling me I'm a helpless bum.

Please listen, not immediately talk or do.
Just listen; that's really what I want from you.
Perhaps that's why prayer is sometimes nice;
God doesn't interrupt with his advice.

Purpose for Interpersonal Verbal Communication

Having a **purpose** for an interpersonal, face-to-face verbal (language) communication is essential in effective listening to one another. (Note the schematic on page 5.) As a listener/reader, one may attend a verbal message for the following purposes (1) to discriminate or distinguish among words and phrases for immediate recall or application, (2) to comprehend, understand or mentally associate presented verbal concepts with those mental concepts that exist in another one's mind, (3) to judge, evaluate, analyze, or interpret the verbal concepts presented, and (4) to relate, associate or empathize with the mental /emotional concept of others.

Note that I am not including appreciative listening skills such as instrumental music. My purpose for this book is to help you understand and improve your interpersonal verbal or language listening skills. I hope that your purpose for reading and experiencing this book is to better understand and improve these skills. To fulfill these purposes, we need to attend a specific message.

Attending, actively being involved and processing of a spoken language message, is the initial step in verbally sharing feeling and thoughts. It is focusing in on and concentrating on one verbal message. Attending is also necessary for effective reading of a message.

I'm reminded of Farmer George and Farmer John. George had a Missouri mule (said to be the most stubborn of animals) that he intended to sell to John. George demonstrated how his mule listened and obeyed each command. John was impressed, purchased the mule and took it home. The next day, John brought the mule back and complained that he could not get the mule to listen to him. George smiled, picked up a board and hit the mule on the head between its two big ears as he said, *"First you have to get its attention before it will listen."*

No, I am not promoting that anyone "thump" anyone else on the head. The skill of effective verbal listening is far more complex than a "thump" on the head, and I am hoping that the story and illustration got your attention. Effective verbal listening requires training and practice; it is not an inherently simple, natural and immediately accomplished task. Some erroneously believe that they are multi-task oriented and can attend and listen to two or more verbal messages at the same time. It is common to observe someone reading a newspaper or typing email while attempting to be listening in a conversation.

Prove to yourself that you can only attend one verbal message at a time by trying to read and comprehend the moving printed news banner at the bottom of the television screen while at the same time listening to the commentator speaking about a different news story. In a "loose conversation," try listening simultaneously to two different people talking about two different topics. You can't make "heads nor tails" from what you hear.

Let's begin this study with a questionnaire on how you perceive yourself as a listener in both interpersonal and lecture listening situations. Put your responses to the questions on a separate sheet of paper. Upon completion of the questionnaire, compare and discuss your responses to each item with your significant other.

Listening Behavior Questionnaire

1. In your interpersonal or social communication, to whom do you listen best? Why do you listen to this person?
2. In your interpersonal or social communication, who is your best listener? Why do you think this person is your best listener?
3. In your interpersonal communication, about what topic do you listen most often and what topic do you find most interesting?
4. In your interpersonal communication, how do you respond when you are listening effectively or indicate that you are listening?
5. In a lecture, sermon or public speech, about what topic or subject matter do you listen most effectively? Why do you listen most effectively to messages about this subject?
6. In a lecture, sermon or public speech, about what topic or subject matter do you listen least effectively? Why do you not listen effectively?
7. How do you respond in a lecture, sermon or public speech when you are listening effectively? (take notes, ask questions, make eye contact with the speaker, facial expressions, body attitude, etc.)
8. In what communication situation, are you most anxious or nervous about listening?
9. What is your most common distraction when you are listening in an interpersonal communication? (the topic, the language, the speaker's appearance, your own tiredness and/or preoccupation, etc.)
10. What is your most common distraction when listening to a lecture or formal speech?

Compare each item of the survey with that of your significant other and discuss.

Listening – A Language Skill

Listening is one of the four language skills. Writing and speaking are the two expressive skills and reading and listening are the two receptive skills. Listening is the first language skill used and the basis of the other language skills' development. However, listening is the least studied formally and most difficult to test or measure. Yet, it is the most admired and respected.

It is said, *"A person would rather marry a poor financial provider than a poor listener,"* and *"No one ever listened him/herself out of a job."*

Following is a schematic of the complex act of spoken interpersonal communication in which the communicators exchange and share speaking and listening roles. Discuss the variables with your significant other. Hopefully, upon completion of the lessons/experiences, you will have far better insight into spoken interpersonal communication and the role of listening.

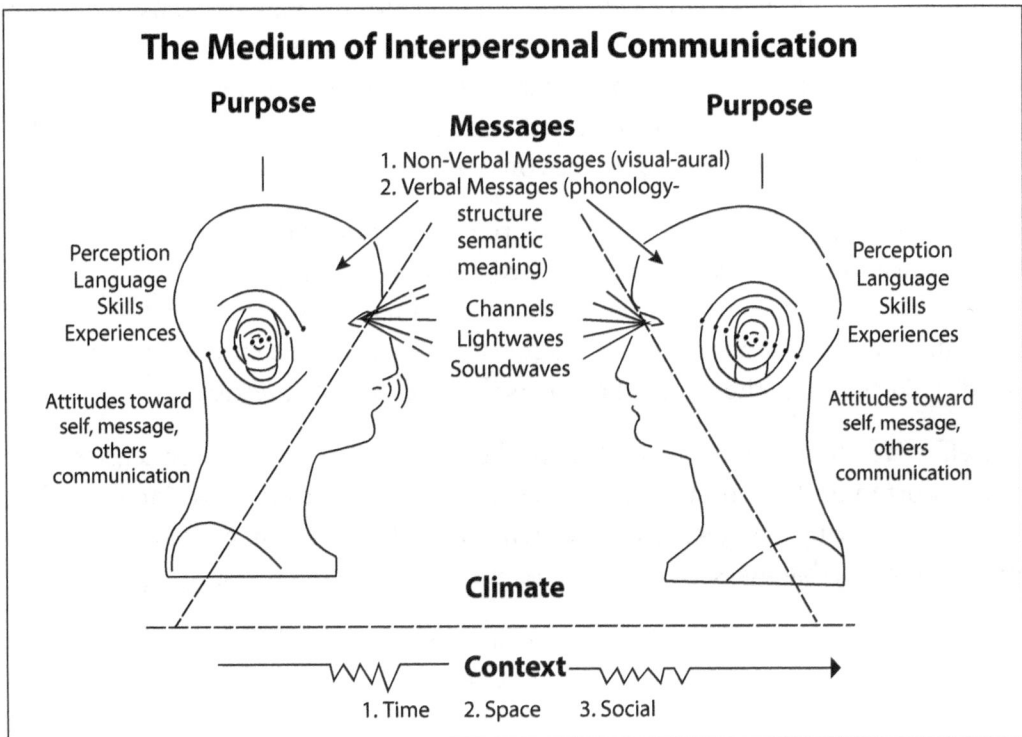

The Medium of Interpersonal Communication

Purpose   **Purpose**

Messages

1. Non-Verbal Messages (visual-aural)
2. Verbal Messages (phonology-structure semantic meaning)

Perception
Language
Skills
Experiences

Channels
Lightwaves
Soundwaves

Perception
Language
Skills
Experiences

Attitudes toward
self, message,
others
communication

Attitudes toward
self, message,
others
communication

Climate

Context

1. Time   2. Space   3. Social

Listening Defined

The International Listening Association defines listening as *"the process of receiving, constructing meaning from and responding to spoken and/or non-verbal messages."* For our purposes we're going to study how to listen to spoken language (verbal) and identify the non-verbal elements that accompany the message.

In the definition, **process** indicates that listening is a complex series of activities and events that are ever changing, ongoing and irreversible. The process begins with an event filled with numerous sensations/stimuli such as sights, sounds, aromas, etc. The listener chooses to hear a spoken verbal message and the accompanying non-verbal elements such as voice inflection, rate, etc. The listener then interprets the words and phrases and makes the association with his/her mental concepts. The listener then draws inferences, generalizes, abstracts and/or concludes from the symbolic mental associations. He/she then responds verbally and/or non-verbally and activates degrees of memory.

> *I know that you understand what you think I said, but I am not sure you realize that what you heard is what I meant.*

Receiving refers to the initial step in the physical listening process. We perceive information about our environment and relationships through our senses: hearing, sight, touch, smell and taste. We all have a sense mode preference; we may prefer to get our information through a particular sense. Some of us prefer to get our verbal messages via the sense of sight (reading); whereas, others prefer hearing them (listening). Some of us have a strong sense of kinesics (doing or touching).

All three of these senses play important roles in face-to-face interpersonal verbal communication; whereas, the printed word, texting, tweeting, Facebook are limited to sight/reading, and telephone and radio are limited to hearing. Touch, a concept difficult to illustrate graphically, plays a role in interpersonal communication via the hand shake, the hug, the hand on the arm/shoulder and/or the kiss.

The effective listener will perceive the speaker's use of all three of these sense modes in an effort to understand the verbal message and the speaker's emotional involvement in delivering that message. Research shows that more than 70 percent of the meaning of a verbal message is in how, when and where the message is presented.

On page 5, the schematic indicates the channels through which we communicate; but, it omits the often important "touch." Only face-to-face interpersonal communication provides the opportunity of perceiving the meaning of a verbal message though the three senses.

Receiving is the selective perception of a communicative message and its accompanying elements from among the many conflicting stimuli. This concept is analogous to my sitting on the bank of a country pond fishing while hundreds of gnats and flies are buzzing around my head vying for my attention. It really bugs me to choose the one or two that I can destroy by trapping them between my clapping hands. Commonly reported distractions include other communicator's appearance, voice or speech pattern, loud physical noise such as (machinery), television, electronic games, texting, others conversing on cell phones or telephone, and your own tiredness or mental preoccupation. Discuss again both your responses to items 9 and 10 on page 3 of the listening behavior self-analysis.

History repeats itself because no one listened at the time.

Constructing meaning is the association in one's mind of words and phrases with references to concepts previously experienced and established. We think in words (symbols) that represent real objects, events or concepts created by words themselves. The word has no direct resemblance or tangible relationship with that which it represents. A word is arbitrarily associated mentally with a particular concept of an object, event, linguistic function or other word, but the word could represent other concepts if we so choose. Check the items under "Messages" in schematic on page 5. Yes, I know all this sounds very academic, but I hope that after discussing it with your significant other, you can get the main idea. The following schematic and example should help. C.K. Ogden and I.A. Richard's **Triangle of Meaning** schematically describes the elements in constructing meaning.

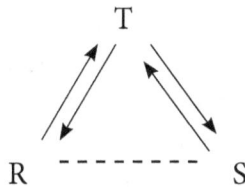

The *referent* R refers to the real world as perceived through the senses and has direct relationship with *thought* (T). The *word* (S, the symbol) is an abstract representation of the *referent* or real world and the *thought*. The lines with the double arrows indicate that the *word* is influenced by *thought* as well as influencing *thought*, and the *referent* is influenced by *thought* as well as influencing *thought*. But there is no real or causal relationship between the *word* and the *referent*. For example, with the word, *cow*, there is no relationship to the animal in the real world and the meaning that is created in the listener's mind or thought. The meanings for the words, *freedom* and *democracy* are very abstract and rely on each listener's mind to create verbal meaning.

The abstraction of language is well demonstrated in the following story: Three under-aged coeds, one from Northwest Missouri State University, one from the University of Missouri and one from Podunk College were at a party where alcohol was served. The police raided the site of the party and the coeds took off running together with the police chasing them. The coeds ran down a no-exit alley, but at the end there were gunnysacks or burlap bags. The girls each got in a different bag to hide. A police officer kicked the bag in which the one from Northwest was hiding. She meowed like a cat and the officer said, *"Nothing but a dumb cat."* He moved on to the bag containing the coed from the University of Missouri and kicked the bag. The coed barked like a dog. The officer exclaimed, *"Nothing but a dumb dog."* He moved on to the sack containing the coed from Podunk College. He kicked it, and she replied, *"POTATOES."* The jig was up!

Responding to spoken verbal and accompanying non-verbal messages is a physiological reaction to what the speaker says and the way he/she says it. The listener's verbal response may be in the form of questions, paraphrased messages or repeated messages. The non-verbal visual responses may be a change in eye behavior, nod of the head, shrug of the shoulders, turning away, smile, change in body attitude or hand gestures.

How did you respond to questions 4 and 6 of the questionnaire on page 3? In our studies of listeners' verbal responses, using the questioner's technique was the most effective in both interpersonal and lecture communications.

In studies of interpersonal communication via questionnaires, the vast majority of young people say their friends are their best listeners (above parents, spouses and siblings). Their friends indicate they are listening by their eye contact and eye referent. By eye contact, we mean short durations of perhaps five seconds and not a stare. Experiment for yourself by looking your significant other in his/her eyes. How long did it take before you became uncomfortable or distracted?

Eye referent indicates whether the person is trying to visualize the referent or concentrating on hearing the language. If a listener is visualizing, he/she will tend to look up and to the left. If a listener is concentrating on the spoken word, he/she will tend to look down and to the right. A listener will indicate attention by a combination of eye contact and eye references. If the listener stares into space you can bet that he/she is not listening.

The visually handicapped person, or someone who is wearing dark-shaded glasses, is at a disadvantage when he/she is responding to a speaker. This is because it is very difficult for the speaker to determine the listener's attitude toward the message and therefore change his/her message. This is especially true in relationship communication where empathy is important.

Facial expressions and body attitude are also important non-verbal visual responses. Do you let the other communicator know how you feel about the subject or his/her behavior by your expressions?

I recall an incident when I began my high school teaching career. I had been given the responsibility for a remedial sophomore English class. These were 15-year-old students who at the age of 16 could quit school and get on with their lives. On the first day the students had gathered and were visiting while I stood at the front of the room looking down at my notes, hoping not to display my anxiety. The bell rang and all the students except for one took their seats.

This young man, who was big for his age, was standing in the doorway leaning on the door frame. I glanced over and perceived his defiant attitude and behavior with the sleeves of his t-shirt rolled up and one bulging as if it were hiding a pack of cigarettes. I said, *"Will you sit down!"* He replied, *"My name ain't Will!"* No matter what I would have said, it would have caused a confrontation and he would get his wish, to be kicked out or suspended from school.

I walked over to him within two feet of him so as not to violate his personal space. I looked him in the eyes and at his face in a non-confronting but interested manner. He took a seat and attended what I said during the class and I was in hog heaven. He was right, his name was Fred, not Will. After class I asked him why he responded to me the way he did. He replied, *"You were the first person that I could remember that showed that you cared by looking at me face-to-face."* Unfortunately, Fred did not find my English class or the rest of his school subjects interesting enough to stay in school after he was 16 years old. He quit to become a gravel truck driver and was killed in an accident shortly thereafter.

With our eyes, facial expression and body attitude, we communicate our feelings and whether we agree, disagree or are indifferent. Please realize how important your response is not only to your own processing of what is being said but also to the speaker.

Listen to others as you would have them listen to you.

Communication Climate

The communication climate as illustrated in the schematic on page 7 significantly influences the effectiveness of the listener. The communication climate reflects the sum of the communicators' attitudes.

Attitudes are classified as positive, negative and indifferent. Each communicator has an attitude toward the other communicator and the subject matter of the message.

If the communicators have positive attitudes toward each other and the subject matter, the communication will be effective and empathetic. If one of the communicators has a negative attitude toward the message or the other communicator, the communication takes place but not as effectively. In these cases, critical listening replaces comprehensive and relationship listening. We also have an attitude toward ourselves in regard to the message and the other communicator.

The following statements represent possible communication climates. Together discuss each one to determine if you perceive the situation as being positive, negative or indifferent.

I always have cared for you, but you are wrong when it comes to the subject of religion.

You don't have the slightest idea what you are talking about.

I love you and I believe in what you say.

I don't care about you or what you have to say.

We have been friends a long time, but I can't agree with you about Tom's unacceptable behavior.

You and your opinions don't matter anyway.

I respect you and we can work this out.

I just can't comprehend your explanation of the process

You have just seen how one's attitude affects the message. All of these attitudes, whether positive, negative or indifferent, make up the feel or the climate that affects how the message is received. The illustration on page 5 shows that climate is the basis or the condition upon which communication evolves.

Types/Purposes for Listening

Discriminative Listening

Discriminative listening is the basic type of listening and it is necessary for the remaining types. Discriminative listening is hearing speech sounds, words or word phrases and classifying them without giving them merit, preference or prejudice. It is the skill of classifying plurals, possessives and degrees (big, bigger, biggest). It is the process of distinguishing similar verbal sounds: *ch* from *sh*, *b* from *p*, *k* from *g*, *f* from *th*, and *v* from *b*.

We are reminded of Fred telling John that he just got a new hearing aid. John asked, *"What kind is it?"* Fred, looking at his watch, replied, *"Half past six."*

Discriminative listening becomes very important in regards to medical terms such as *oncology, laparoscopic, aphasia* and a plethora of others, including drug names such as Prevacid, Procrit, Plavix, Prachol and Protonix. Many times I have been asked what medicine I am taking, but I cannot answer that question because I didn't listen well when it was introduced to me. I'd be in trouble if I got my "P" medicine mixed up.

It is the same way in remembering someone's name after a verbal introduction. One has to discriminate before one can remember another's name.

Discriminative listening also involves hearing and recalling numerical information such as social security numbers, telephone numbers, zip codes, etc. When you check out at the grocery store, the clerk tells you the amount due and you respond appropriately. There is a fine line that separates discriminative listening and comprehensive listening. When one manipulates the numbers through addition, subtraction and multiplication, it is comprehensive listening.

Discriminative listening distinguishes moods, attitudes and feelings. These are expressed through voice inflections, tempo, how loud and soft one speaks and other visual cues. The same verbal phrase can be expressed in several ways through which the meaning is changed. The way the speaker says, *Stop it,* indicates the degree of certainty the speaker intends. If the speaker prolongs the phrase with a rising pitch inflection, he/she lacks assertiveness and certainty. It also causes questions in regards to the speaker's intent.

Discriminative listening is determining the denotative or dictionary meaning of a word according to its verbal context. The word, *fast* has 20 different dictionary meanings depending on its verbal context and situation. If a female is referring to a male by saying, *He is really fast,* does she mean on the running track?

Your ears don't work until your tongue expires!

Discriminative Listening Experience #1

One significant other reads the message and asks the questions. The other(s) listens and responds. Do one at a time and discuss. Exchange speaker/listener role after item 10.

1. Mary's mother has four children: two boys and two girls. All the children are named after saints. The boys' names are Peter and John. One of the girls is named Elizabeth.

    What is the other daughter's name?

2. *Most untrained listeners will comprehend only 25 percent of what has been said.*

    What percentage of what is said is comprehended by the untrained listeners?

3. The audiologist, observing the client's inconsistent and inaccurate responses to the "pure tone" audiometric test, labeled the client as a malingerer.

    What does 'malingerer' mean?

4. Sit down, stand up, look to your left, put your right hand on the top of your head while you say "oops," and then put your left index finger in your left ear, frown and sit down.

    a. *What were you to have said?*
    b. *What direction were you to have looked?*
    c. *What were the first and last things you were to do?*
    d. *What were you to have done with your index finger?*

5. Cherry, shalom, sherry, church.

    a. *What word represents a type of wine?*
    b. *What two words have the initial sound of 'ch'?*
    c. *What two words have the initial sound of 'sh'?*
    d. *What word represents a Jewish greeting?*

6. Attending difficulties in the listening process include 1) environmental distractions, 2) inability to respond, 3) mental preoccupation, 4) hearing difficulties, and 5) indifferent attitude.

    What are three of the five 'attending' difficulties in the listening process?

7. John's voice is loud, Julie's voice is louder, Joe's voice is loudest.

    a. *Whose voice is loudest?*
    b. *Whose voice is louder than the other two?*
    c. *Whose voice has the least intensity?*

8. In the series of numbers: 2, 4, 7, 6, 8.

   a. What is the fourth number?
   b. What is the only odd number?
   c. What is the sum of the first two numbers?

9. Write the standard English for the following statements.

   "Where da ya cum frum?" "Who's dat ober dar?"

10. What does 'skirt' mean in the following statement?
    "Do not skirt your responsibilities."

    a. a garment
    b. fringe
    c. evade
    d. fulfill

Change speaker/listener roles.

1. There is a dead frog sitting on a lily pad. The lily pad is five feet from the pond's west bank, three feet from the north bank, eight feet from the east bank and ten feet from the south bank.

   "Which way should the frog jump to reach the closest bank?" (none; the frog is dead)

2. Listening involves the senses of hearing, sight and sometimes touch, but hearing is the primary sense involved and can serve alone.

   What is the primary sense involved in listening?

3. Listening is a learned, intended and self-generated behavior that is not spontaneous in nature.

   What does 'spontaneous' mean?

4. Raise your right arm above your head, clinch a fist with your left hand, place your left clinched fist on your right elbow, raise your right foot about an inch off the floor, smile and say "Good job."

   a. What was your second instruction?
   b. How high should you raise your right foot above the floor?
   c. What were you to have said?
   d. What was your first instruction?

5. Preparing to listen includes a) having a purpose, b) having prior knowledge or awareness of the subject, c) having an interest in or ability to relate to the topic and d) being ready and capable of listening.

   What are the steps in preparing to listen?

6. Ted is listening to the recorded speech now; yesterday, Mary listened to the recorded speech; tomorrow Fred will listen to the recorded speech; Alice could have listened to the speech at any of those times.

   In a sentence write down when each of the individuals experienced listening to the recorded speech.

7. In the series of numbers: 1, 7, 3, 2, 7.

   a. *What number is repeated?*
   b. *What is the only even number?*
   c. *What is the third number in the series?*

8. Jane's telephone number is 660-582-4682; Harry's telephone number is 402-625-3827; George's telephone number is 660-562-4150.

   a. *Which two numbers have the same area code?*
   b. *What is Harry's telephone number?*

9. Margaret was in trouble because she threw away the rough draft of her paper.
   "Draft" used here means?

   a. *Selected*
   b. *Check*
   c. *Preliminary version*
   d. *Air flow*

10. In the series of words: coat, cap, orange, gloves and boots.

    a. *What is the fourth word?*
    b. *What word's referent does not fit the category of the others?*
    c. *What two words in the series are plural?*
    d. *What word in the series represents the largest item?*

Discriminative Listening Experience #2

The first speaker reads the first four messages and asks questions to be answered by the first listener individually. Change speaker/listener roles for second four messages.

1. The telephone number is 816-573-2406. Note the area code is Kansas City.

   What is the telephone number?

2. When entering the town on Highway 46 from the west, proceed five blocks to Munn Street. Turn right onto South Munn and go three blocks and turn left on Cooper Street. Your destination is the third house on your right.

   Repeat the directions given.

3. Charlie is 5 foot 8 inches tall and weighs 170 pounds; he has brown hair and blue eyes. He has a distinguishing tattoo of a heart with an arrow piercing it on his right forearm.

   Repeat the description.

4. Recipe for healthy potato soup: One package of frozen shredded potatoes, four cans of fat-free chicken broth and one package of fat-free gravy mix. Combine potatoes and broth and simmer for 10 minutes. Dissolve gravy mix in one-half cup of water and add to simmering potatoes and broth, continue to simmer mixture for 15 minutes.

   Repeat the healthy potato soup recipe.

Change roles.

1. When entering the city from the west on Highway 46, proceed eight blocks to Main Street and the first stop light. Turn left and go four blocks north on Main, just after you pass the courthouse, turn right and continue on Fourth Street three blocks. Your destination is the fifth building on the left.

   Listener is to repeat instructions.

2. Mildred is 5 foot 6 inches tall, weighs 130 pounds and she has blond hair and blue eyes. She has a dimpled chin and a light complexion. She has a slight brown birthmark on the right side of her neck.

   Repeat the description.

3. The listening process involves attending, sensing, evaluating, interpreting and responding.

   Repeat the five steps in the listening process.

4. The telephone number is 660-582-7530; the area code includes Skidmore Missouri.

   Repeat the telephone number.

Discriminative Listening Experience #3

Discriminative listening is the immediate distinction and recall of a series of words, phrases, numerical values, comparative degrees, verb tenses, plural and possessive nouns and semantic elements and is distinguished from comprehensive listening that requires mental association, analysis and understanding. This distinction is illustrated with the following experience. One partner reads the following items and the listener responds to the question.

1. In the series of numbers 5, 7, 10, 13, 2,

    What is the third number?

2. In the series of numbers 8, 6, 4, 10, 2, a series of even numbers,

    What is the second number?

3. In the series of letters Y, A, V, C, N, Z, a series of six letters,

    What is the second to the last letter?

4. In the series of nouns COW, MOUSE, PIG, HORSE, CHICKEN, DOG,

    What is the fourth noun?

5. In the series of words ON, FOR, TO, AND, THE, A. These are function words. They do not have an emotional reaction or semantic meaning. They are used to tie the content words and phrases together. Function words include articles, conjunctions, prepositions and sometimes adverbs. An isolated function word such as *the* creates no mental concept other than the word itself; whereas, the content word, *cow*, creates a mental image immediately. Function words are used to make up phrases and sentences. *Tweeters* often leave function words out of their messages assuming that the receiver of the message can establish the relationship of the content words. Function words tie our language together.

    Write the third word in the series. Now, write as completely as you can the message I just gave you about function words. More than likely the listener will recall "TO" as the third word of the series but will be unable to recall more than 15 words of the 100 used to describe a "function word." You have now experienced the difference between "discriminative" and "comprehensive" listening.

Comprehensive Listening

Comprehensive listening combines and associates spoken language concepts discriminately being heard with verbal concepts already established in the mind or memory. It is the process of understanding or giving meaning to the spoken verbal message and its accompanying non-verbal cues. Comprehensive listening depends on discriminative listening and is necessary for critical listening.

Comprehensive listening is the act of interpreting the spoken language messages. These messages are then associated with the memory of real or vicarious experiences. The receiver then responds without prejudice to that association either covertly or overtly through paraphrasing or asking questions. This is the most important type of listening.

Listening is an instantaneous dynamic process in which concepts cannot be retrieved. Listening without questioning is like the axiom, *You can't step in the same stream twice.*

The advantage of listening is that one does have the opportunity to ask questions and should. One's interest in a subject is determined by his/her prior experience and vocabulary in regards to the subject. It is interesting to note that when one is to speak or write on a subject, he/she becomes more familiar with the subject. One would certainly hesitate to speak on a topic, about which he/she knew little.

In a school setting, the incentive for comprehensive listening is to extract important information from the teacher. The incentive for listening to significant others is to understand them better. This is important in building good interpersonal relationships.

One should also prepare to listen both comprehensively and critically. To illustrate this principle, read aloud the following narrative poem by E. A. Robinson. (One reads, the other listens.)

How Annandale Went Out
by E. A. Robinson

They called it Annandale — and I was there
To flourish, to find words, and to attend:
Liar, physician, hypocrite, and friend,
I watched him, and the sight was not so fair
As one or two that I have seen elsewhere:
An apparatus not for me to mend —
A wreck, with hell between him and the end,
Remained of Annandale, and I was there.

I knew the ruin as I knew the man,
So put the two together, if you can,
Remembering the worst you know of me.
Now view yourself as I was, on the spot —
With a slight kind of engine. Do you see?
Like this ... You wouldn't hang me? I thought not.

More than likely, you were unable to comprehend it. Now reread the poem knowing that the speaker of the message is speaking from the gallows about to be hanged for the murder of his friend, Annandale. You may still have difficulty understanding some of the word phrases, but at least you have gained insight into the controversial topic of euthanasia (mercy killing).

Comprehensive Listening Experience #1

One significant other reads aloud, as if he/she were speaking, the message to the second "significant other" who listens and responds to the questions asked. Discuss the answers.

Of the four language skills (listening, reading, speaking, and writing) listening is the primary or first to be developed. Just as a Native-American first learns to listen to his language, so must one who is learning a language as a second language. Listening is the basis of the progressive sequence and interdependence among the receptive (listening and reading) and expressive (speaking and writing) language skills. The direct influence of listening on reading has not been proven conclusively, but it appears that our reading skill is normally superimposed on our listening base and our ability to listen determines our ability to read. Whether or not reading is a special extension of the thought process established in listening is not known, but there is a significant relationship of the two language skills and the importance of learning to listen to a language before learning to read that language has been established.

1.   *What are the four language skills and explain what they are?*

2.   *Explain how you perceive listening to language to be different from listening to music.*

3.   *What are the receptive language skills and how are they related to the expressive language skills?*

Exchange speaker/listener roles.

The relationship of listening and the first learned expressive language skill, speaking, is obvious. The deaf who are unable to listen are also unable to develop or maintain spoken language. The child learns to speak communicatively by listening to himself and others. However, if the ability and incentive for listening is not present, the development of speech does not occur.

The relationship of listening to writing is less pronounced, but listening skill appears to influence writing. This is especially apparent in regard to vocabulary imagery and language syntax, or the pattern of sentences or phrases. Those who have the ability to listen use a larger number of words in their writing. They can distinguish and use subtle tones of meaning. Their sentences tend to be more complex, qualifying and comprehendable.

It is apparent from experience and research that listening is the primary language skill upon which the other language skills of speaking, reading and writing are sequentially developed.

1.   *Explain the relationship of listening in the development of speaking.*

2.   *Explain the relationship of listening in the development of writing.*

3.   *Explain why listening is the primary language skill.*

Comprehensive Listening Experience #2

The speaker is to read the following aloud, after which he/she is to ask the three requests individually and discuss each.

What is the listening process and what are its component parts? The first essential part of listening is hearing. This is the physical process of changing sound waves into nerve impulses. In language listening, auditory discrimination of phonemes or individual sounds of a language is essential and difficult to develop. Hearing is influenced by physical environment and physiological abilities. Since communication with our environment is through our senses (sight, taste, touch, smell and hearing) simultaneously, we may be overwhelmed by the other senses' stimuli and not hear the words. Or we may have an organic defect that prevents the changing of sound waves, to vibration and nerve impulses. The organic defect may occur within the eardrum, middle ear bones, or sensory nerve damage in the inner ear.

Requested listener responses.

1. Describe the physical hearing process.

2. Describe what may cause difficulty in hearing.

3. Describe what the auditory discrimination of phonemes is.

Comprehensive Listening Experience #3

The speaker of the last experience becomes the listener and answers the following questions and discusses them with the speaker after hearing the information read aloud.

Another important variable or element of the listening process is that of past experience with the language. Another variable is the perception of the referents which are symbolized by the language's words. A person has to experience through his/her sense or be able to relate it to another experience in order to process a word such as *fire* as a concept. If one has not had any experience in reference to a word or cannot acquire meaning for a word from its context, the process of comprehensive listening does not take place.

The listener's attitudes toward the message, the speaker, and him/herself play an important role in listening. In order for critical listening to take place, the listener must have a positive or negative feeling toward the existing communication. One who is indifferent to his environment cannot listen attentively and critically.

Listening is a learned, involving, and active process that includes hearing, attending, interpreting, concept association, auditory memory, and response. Learn to listen and you will be able to listen to learn.

Requested listener responses:

1. *Explain the role of the listener's past experiences in comprehensive listening.*

2. *Explain the role of attitudes in comprehensive listening.*

3. *Explain comprehensive listening.*

Organization in Comprehensive Listening

Comprehensive listening involves determining the organization pattern of the spoken message in order to process it in one's mind. The listener must recognize if the pattern is according to chronological order, spatial order, categorical order, causes to effect, or problem/solution (nature of the problem, causes of the problem, possible solutions, best solution and how to put into effect).

If the speaker's organization pattern is not recognizable, the listener must create his/her own. When experiencing a lengthy or extended spoken message such as a lecture, it is advantageous for the listener to establish an organization pattern and take written notes. Check how you answered number 7 on the self-analysis questionnaire on page 3.

The speaker usually will use the chronological pattern when referring to narratives and historical perspective messages. Written notes will help the listener reestablish the message's events in dates or time after immediate recall passes with time.

When listening to an extended message dealing with physical characteristics, he/she should take notes according to the space relationship (the hip bone is connected to the thigh bone, the thigh bone is connected to the knee bone). The categorical organization is often used in note taking to comprehend biological or literary topics through identifying species and genre. This note taking organizational pattern is used particularly in discussion listening.

Discriminative listening is the prerequisite to comprehensive listening. Comprehensive listening is prerequisite to critical listening.

Comprehensive Listening Organization Experiences 1 through 4

The first significant other reads experiences 1 and 3 with immediate answering by second significant other through questions and discussion. The significant others change roles for experiences 2 and 4. Listener note taking is permitted.

1. The listening process involves receiving a spoken message through the senses of hearing and sight. The meaning of the message is abstracted and reconstructed in the listener's mind after which the listener responds verbally and/or non-verbally based on his/her interpretation of the message.

    a. Paraphrase the message's content.
    b. What organizational pattern did you use in your paraphrasing?

2. Sound waves enter the ear through the auditory canal and then these sound waves cause the ear drum to vibrate. The vibration causes the tiny bones in the middle ear to change the waves to mechanical action which affects the membrane of the oval window. The oval window creates a flow of fluid in the inner ear cochlea and the flow of fluid excites certain nerve cells which send the message to the brain.

    a. Paraphrase the message's content.
    b. What organizational pattern did you use in your paraphrasing?

3. The listening process involves selecting, attending, interpreting, associating, and responding/remembering. The selection of the message is based on your purpose for listening. After selecting, attending, interpreting and associating the listener responds/remembers.

    a. Paraphrase the message content.
    b. What organizational pattern did you use in your paraphrasing?

4. Listening is most effective if the speaker first makes eye contact with the listener, then the speaker addresses the listener by name, and relates a message to the listener. It is best if the speaker uses positive words and most importantly uses vocal variety in his/her delivery of the message.

    a. Paraphrase the message.
    b. What organizational pattern did you use?

Comprehensive Listening Experience #5

Listen to comprehend and solve the problem presented in the message.

One participant reads the following message to the other participant(s): It has been estimated that over 80 percent of American teenagers do not communicate with their parents about sexuality, and they learn this topic from "experienced" peers. Researchers attribute the lack of parental/child communication about sexuality to: 1) using euphemisms or substitute words with children for genitals, birth and eliminations, 2) the association of sexuality with being negative, dirty or very personal, and 3) the association of sexuality with guilt and sin.

Unfortunately, because of lack of communication about sexuality, teenagers learn from experiences rather than listening to their parents. Even the teenagers do not verbally communicate about sexuality when dating because *sex* isn't something to discuss. Thus, the experiences end in unwanted pregnancies or the spread of venereal diseases.

   a. *Paraphrase the message.*
   b. *What organizational pattern did you use?*

Comprehensive Listening Experience #6

A significant other reads as if giving a lecture; listener is to listen and take notes and ask two questions before responding to the separate questions.

Storytelling is a language art akin to oratory and parables. It usually involves a narrative that is expressed orally in a live person–to-person context that has both the teller and the listener involved in an empathetic or understandable communication. Storytelling is like oratory in that it usually is presented orally without a script, but the purpose and the language styles are different. Oratory expresses a message intended for a critical listener and is delivered in a formal language style; whereas, storytelling is intended for an empathetic listener and is delivered in a colloquial or folksy style.

Storytelling, like the parable, is presented orally without a script. Although storytelling may have a moral message, its main purpose is to entertain. This is often done by making fun of oneself and/or regional or rural folks of the past. It requires empathetic listeners.

Listener responds to each question separately after which listener and speaker discuss listeners' responses.

1. *Compare storytelling to other language arts.*

2. *What makes storytelling a unique language art?*

3. *Paraphrase the message using comparison/contrast organization.*

Comprehensive Listening Experience #7

The significant other speaker now becomes the listener who may take notes and ask questions before responding to the inquiries below.

The topics for storytelling usually involve rural folks, backwoods folks, imaginative characters or deprecating behavior of one's self. In other words, it is making fun of backward or naive behaviors.

The requisites of storytelling are that it must appeal to the senses and excite the imagination in both the language and presentation. It uses figures of speech in the language and voice inflection/pauses and gestures in the presentation. Figures of speech that appeal to the senses include: 1) alliteration – *little, lively lily; Myron Mukie met Mildred Mukie in the middle of the meet,* 2) assonance – *now never mind me; didn't do diddley; the murmuring of the miserable mourners; the purple curtain created turmoil,* and 3) repetition/refrain – *I should have known.*

Figures of speech that excite the imagination include: 1) power of suggestion – *a thinly clad person or concept is more sensuous than a naked person or outright comment,* 2) metaphor/simile – *swings like a rusty gate,* 3) allegorical – characters' names represent principles being promoted – *Sargent Pride and Private Humble, Mercury Mukie,* 4) hyperbole – obvious exaggeration – His arms dangled a mile out of his sleeves. He hit the ball a country mile. 5) dialogue – *He said to his partner, Did you wanta go? Hell, no was the reply.* and 6) direct address – *Ya know what I mean!*

Requested listener responses:

1. *What are figures of speech?*

2. *How do figures of speech appeal to the senses and excite the imagination?*

3. *Paraphrase using categorical organization patterns.*

Comprehensive Listening Experience #8

Significant others exchange speaker and listener roles. Listener is encouraged to take notes and ask questions before responding to questions below.

When telling a story the requirements are that the message must appeal to the senses and excite thought and imagination. To accomplish these, the *teller* must consider both audible and visual non-verbal expressions. Audible elements are 1) voice pitch inflections (a rising pitch indicates question or doubt and humor; lowering the pitch indicates certainty and assertiveness), 2) voice intensity or loudness (increase in intensity indicates importance or significance), 3) speech rhythm, rate and pauses (used for emphasis or attention and suggestion of audience's perspective) and 4) expletives or non-verbal sounds such as *Oh, Oops and Ok*, (adds informality).

Visual elements include: 1) eye contact/referent (indicates empathy or the sharing of feelings, and referent reflects the communicator's thought), 2) facial expressions – eyebrows, forehead, lips (indicate communicator's attitude, emotions and involvement in the topic), 3) hand gestures (indicate reaching out for touch and demonstrating descriptions) and 4) body attitude (indicates involvement with other communicators).

Listener responds to requests and discussion of each item.

1. *Explain audible non-verbal and how they involve the communicators.*

2. *Explain visual non-verbal and how they involve the communicators.*

Critical Listening

In the hierarchy of verbal listening, after the listener discriminates the words and phrases and comprehends the message, he/she may choose to listen critically. This means to listen with the purpose of evaluation and judgment of the message.

Credibility

The first element in evaluation is the perception of the speaker's credibility. Is the speaker trustworthy and one to whom you would give the keys to your car? Or is he/she one whose *dog hesitates to come when he/she calls it to dinner?*

We evaluate others on their 1) knowledge, wisdom, experience and/or expertise, 2) their character or predictable behavior and 3) their goodwill or caring about the listener and the subject. It would be a waste of your time to listen critically to a person who indicates that he/she knows little about the subject and really doesn't care. That carries over in many of our communication situations.

One certainly would not critically listen to a guy who has his *medium-sized pizza cut into six pieces instead of eight because he doesn't think he could eat eight.* Nor would one critically listen to the guy who consistently *changes his residence because he heard that most auto accidents happen within five miles of home.*

In a communication situation, the listener creates an attitude toward the speaker and the message. The speaker creates an attitude toward the listener and the message. If the speaker indicates either a negative or positive attitude toward either the listener or the subject, critical listening may take place even though the two communicators' attitudes do not have to be the same. It is only when the speaker or listener has no attitude toward the other communicator or subject and is indifferent, that critical listening cannot occur. Therefore, it is necessary for the listener to develop an interest and an attitude toward the speaker and the message in order to listen critically.

In the old days, if one heard it on the radio or read it in the newspaper it was obviously perceived as accurate truth. Now we make that mistake with Facebook, Google and Twitter and other social media.

Critical Listening Credibility Experience #1

Together discuss if and why you would listen and believe what the speaker would say about the given topic.

1. *A nationally-known professional football player who does not know you personally is attempting to persuade you about the benefits of solar panel energy.*

2. *A military veteran whom you do not know personally wishes to speak to you about donating funds to the group that purchases gifts for hospitalized veterans.*

3. *A friend whom you have met on Facebook wishes to speak to you person-to-person about her chosen religion.*

4. *A Ph.D. in geology wishes to speak to you about the dangers in shale fracturing for natural gas.*

5. *Your significant other is speaking to you about saving money.*

Critical Listening Credibility Experience #2

Significant other speaker in #1 now becomes listener. Listener will answer questions orally and discuss the correctness of the answer with the speaker.

According to Pamela Cooper, Ph.D., a nationally-known communication consultant for business and industry, the most important skill that a salesperson should have is listening. Clients or customers report that a salesperson's listening skill is manifested in his/her ability *to* attend or respond through eye contact and other non-verbal elements, by repeating or paraphrasing what the client says, and asking good questions. Listening is more important than the presentation of material (the pitch) and the closing of the sale.

1. *What is the source of the information?*

2. *What question would you ask about the source or attribution?*

3. *What is a salesperson's most important skill?*

4. *How is this skill demonstrated?*

Statement of Fact, Inference and Implied/Opinion

The critical listener must distinguish among statements of facts, inferences and implications (opinions). He/she needs to evaluate the supporting evidence provided.

Factual Statement

A factual statement is based on information that exists outside the minds of the speaker and listener. It associates concepts that are verifiable or replicated experiences. Factual statements are based on events of the past, existing objects, conditions and/or events, public accepted statements or maxims. A factual statement is an unqualified statement in the form of *Something is...* or *Something does...* . It does not contain hypothetical auxiliary verbs such as *could, should, may, would* or the conditional words *if* and *perhaps*, or the qualifying clause, *I think...* .

Inference

An inference is a statement that comes from an association with a fact or experience. You might think what is true in the factual statement is true in the associated statement. It has a logical basis that can be inductive (association of specific to the general) or deductive (association of the general to a specific). If a concept is the same as a fact or group of facts, what is true with one will be true with the others. The critical listener must be alert to the reasoning process involved in the association.

Implied/Opinion

An implied statement evolves from a bias source or opinion. It is general and abstract, relying significantly on what is thought or known about the subject. It is hypothetical and figurative in nature. Acceptance of the implied statement relies on the credibility of the source. An inference has a tangible or direct association with a fact, whereas, an implied statement is indirectly associated. The following story is intended to illustrate the differences among factual, inferred, and implied statements.

> A little boy was out digging a hole in his backyard when the neighbor came over to inquire what the little boy was digging. The little boy told the neighbor that his canary had died (a fact) and he was going to bury it (an inference). The neighbor asked, "*Why do you need such a large box and large hole for your little canary?*" (implying that the boy was wasting time and energy). The little boy replied, "*The fact is I needed a big box and a big hole because my canary is inside your big, dumb, dead cat.*"

Critical Listening for Facts, Inferences and Opinions Experience #1

We define *fact* as a statement that reports an event as it is described through the senses and can be verified or corroborated. An *inference* is defined as an interpretation, prediction or derived theory about the unknown from the known or fact. An opinion/supposition is a statement that goes beyond what can be observed or legitimately inferred and adds an evaluation, generalization or judgment within the statement. One significant other reads a statement aloud in <u>no particular</u> order in the series and the listener is to categorize the statement as *fact, opinion* or *inference*. Discuss after each response. Switch speaker/listener roles after six series.

John is wearing a wedding ring. (F)   John is wearing a wedding band, he must be married. (I)   John's wife must be a real ding-a-ling. (O)

Susan is a fair-skinned person. (F)   Apparently, Susan sunburns easily.(I)   I think Susan is unhealthy. (O)

Fred is a student at this university. (F)   Since Fred is a student at this university, he must have scored above 23 on the ACT. (I).   Fred is a very smart guy. (O)

Elaine has looked at her watch three times. (F)   Since Elaine looks at her watch often, she must have another appointment. (I).   Obviously, Elaine is a very poor listener. (O)

It is raining and the windows of my car are down. (F)   Because it is raining, the seats in my car will get wet. (I)   I'm the unluckiest guy in the world. (O)

Joe has a fever. (F)   Because Joe has a fever, he must be ill. (I)   Joe sure looks sick to me. (O)

Change speaker/listener roles.

Pete was at the bar last night from 9 p.m. to midnight. (F)   At the bar last night, Pete visited with other people. (I).   Pete's a drunk, you know. (O)

Janet is an immoral person. (O)   Janet is pregnant. (F)   Because Janet is pregnant, she must be married. (I)

Bob smiled at me today when we met. (F)   Bob is a happy old fart.(O)   Bob was pleased to see me as he smiled when we met. (I)

Bill is a very careless person. (O)   Bill's house is on fire. (F)   Someone or something caused the fire at Bill's house. (I)

I am speaking. (F)   Since I am speaking, you must be listening. (I)   You are a good listener. (O)

The wind is blowing at a rate of 75-miles-an-hour. (F)   With a 75-mile-an-hour wind, the ripe wheat will be damaged. (I)   This is one helluva storm. (O)

Critical Listening in Distinguished Facts, Inferences, and Opinions Experiences #2

One significant other reads aloud while the other listens and then answers the questions asked.

Deborah Tannen, Ph.D. has stated in her textbook that much of the *office conversations* deal with sports and that females are left out because females are not into *sports talk*. Tannen further states that *small talk* about sports often determines who is favored and promoted within the company. Because women are not interested in sports and do not use sport clichés (idioms) they are often left out of the office hierarchy.

Bob Bohlken, Ph.D., disagrees with Tannen's statements that women are not interested in sports and that they do not know *sports talk* or use sports clichés. Bohlken, to prove his point, gave a list of 36 baseball idioms (i.e. *He struck out with her, She is out in right field, Caught way off base*,) to 40 women and 40 men between the ages of 19 and 30 years. The results are that the females averaged 66 percent knowledgeable and the males averaged 68 percent knowledgeable. There may be a difference but it doesn't appear significant and Tannen's speculations are unfounded.

The speaker reads the following questions aloud and the listener responds out loud with the answer being a fact, an inference or an opinion.

1. *Office conversations center around sports. (O)*

2. *Females are not included in office conversations. (O)*

3. *Since females do not talk about sports, they are excluded from office conversations. (I)*

4. *Tannen stated that woman are not interested in sports. (F)*

5. *Tannen stated that women are left out of the office hierarchy. (F)*

6. *Bohlken gave a list of 36 baseball idioms to 40 males and 40 females for evaluation. (F)*

7. *The study's sample age group represents society. (O)*

8. *Because the difference in the responses of the male and female did not vary significantly, males and females know sports language equally well. (I)*

9. *"He's way off base" is a sports idiom. (F)*

10. *Because there was no significant difference, males and females equally share an interest in sports. (I)*

Critical Listening Language Usage Considerations

Facts, inferences and implications are based on the use of language. There are five important considerations or elements of critical verbal listening awareness: 1) quantification, 2) degrees of abstraction and specificity, 3) attribution, 4) qualified statements, and 5) comparison.

Quantification

The critical listener must be aware of the speaker's use of quantification. There are two types of quantifiers – precise numerical concepts and pseudo quantifying terms.

Precise numerical and absolute terms can be conceptualized and analyzed by the listener. They include numbers, fractions, percentages and words that represent complete or total quantities such as *none, all, everyone, nothing,* and specific references to time and date *3 PM, January 14, 1935.* Precise quantifiers possess a set standard value that can be directly appraised and compared.

Pseudo quantifiers represent that which only seem to be or appear to be measurable or numerable but which are deceptive resemblances. Pseudo quantifiers provide no specific comparable or tangible referent of a set, standard value.

Pseudo quantifiers include *many, several, few, majority, large, small, limited, much, more, thousands, scores, lots,* and *very large crowd.* If the speaker uses precise quantifications the listener accepts or rejects the data; however, if the speaker uses pseudo quantification, the listener needs to question the data.

Some of the polls stated she won, is a pseudo or quasi-quantified statement. *Three of the five polls' results stated she won,* is a concrete or real quantified statement.

Critical Listening Quantification Experience

One significant other reads the first four statements and the listener answers whether the statement contains a *real quantifier* or a *pseudo quantifier*. Discuss each separate item.

1. *That behavior was not acceptable in the olden days. (pseudo)*

2. *None of the contestants won an award. (real)*

3. *Several of his friends on Facebook recommended her. (pseudo)*

4. *Everyone in the group witnessed the crime, but no one would testify. (real)*

Switch speaker/listener roles.

1. *Many in the large crowd approved of her selection. (pseudo)*

2. *Three of the five polls taken showed a significant difference. (real)*

3. *On December 7, 1941, the Japanese attacked Pearl Harbor. (real)*

4. *Scores of people are starving to death in Africa. (pseudo)*

Degree of Abstraction/Specificity

Language is symbolic and inherently abstract. The critical listener needs to be aware of the degree of abstraction and specificity. He/she also needs to distinguish perceivable and specific concepts from intangible and general concepts. Examples of abstract terms are *freedom, beauty, justice, honor, liberal, conservative,* and *religion,* all of which have more than 10 denotations and far more individual connotations.

Abstractness is associated with the context in which the meaning of a word is developed and experienced. When the critical listener hears figurative language the message is more interesting but less specific, concrete or objective.

If you as a critical listener were to *keep your ear to the ground* and *don't let this message go in one ear and out the other* you would have to guess what I was implying. You would not take it literally.

Vernacular or jargon is another element of abstraction of which the critical listener must be aware. Consider these two examples: 1) Because of the physician's therapeutic misadventure and incomplete success in treating the ballistically induced aperture of the subcutaneous environment, the patient experienced a terminal episode. (Because the physician failed to treat the bullet wound appropriately the patient died.) 2) Take your portable hand-held communication inscriber and provide this fiscal underachiever with a financial remuneration expression. (Take your pen and write the poor person a check.)

Remember the poem **How Annandale Went Out** by E.A. Robinson on page 19. This piece of narrative poetry relies on abstract word usage. It gets the listener/reader involved in determining the meaning of the message. However, the message does not clearly express the writer's intent of the message for the critical listener.

Critical Listening Abstraction/Specificity Experience

One significant other reads/speaks the first four items and the listener responds as to the degree of abstractness of an individual item during a discussion with the speaker/listener. Exchange speaker and listener roles for the second four items.

1.   *Only a heathen liberal would even discuss that issue.*

2.   *Our enemy is terrorism.*

3.   *The identified Jim Jones committed the murder.*

4.   *In reference to Ethel, "The old gray mare is not what she used to be."*

Switch speaker/listener roles.

1.   *"Beauty is in the eyes of the beholder."*

2.   *"He wears the hat but he ain't got the cattle."*

3.   *I saw Ed slap Ellen's face.*

4.   *Those Nazi skin-heads allegedly started the fight.*

Attribution

Attribution is giving recognition and credit for a source's quoted information other than the speaker's own message. The critical listener needs to be aware of the source of the message.

We have already discussed the listener's responsibility to determine the speaker's credibility; it is also necessary to evaluate the credibility of the other sources quoted by the speaker. This is especially true in listening to formal public speakers and lecturers. The listener must judge the expertise, standards and goodwill of the quoted source, the time and context of the sources' presented material and the validity of the numerical data presented.

For example, the listener must evaluate whether Peyton Manning is a better judge than anyone else of Pappa John's Pizza; or, if Kimberly Batty-Herbert knows anything about the pistol formation in football. In these two cases the source's expertise should be evaluated.

Another consideration of the quoted sources is whether expressed information is current or from the past. Opinions, perspectives and survey statistics change rapidly; in this electronic world even what was said last week may be outdated. Both the verbal and physical contexts of the quoted material are concerns of the critical listener.

 In the verbal context, the quoted material may be taken as a small portion of the original message. For example, the original message may have said, *The film was awful, but the acting was outstanding* and it may have been quoted .... *Acting was outstanding.* The real or physical context of the quoted material may have been for a different purpose and audience. The quoted material may have been from a speech by a lawyer to a jury, but was used in a speech critical of the freedom of speech.

The validity of numerical data should be the concern of the critical listener. Numerical data is often reported in percentages, not the most reliable and valid measure. The size and nature of the sample should always be considered: *Three out of four people interviewed are against legalizing abortion.* A critical listener should question how many people were interviewed.

Critical Listening Attribution Experience

One significant other reads/speaks the first four items and the listener discusses his/her evaluation of the individual item as to the credibility of the attributing source. Change speaker/listener roles for second four items.

1. *It has been said on Facebook that we will have a drought this summer.*

2. *An official, unofficially, reported that drugs may have been involved.*

3. *Congressman Chris Bond said publicly that he will introduce the listening legislation in the House of Representatives.*

4. *Melissa Beal, Professor of Communications at Northern Iowa University, says research shows that listening is the basis of the other language skills.*

Switch speaker/listener roles.

1. *Twitter is buzzing with the truth about the matter according to Sheila Bentley.*

2. *Andrew Wolvin, Professor of Communication at Maryland University, states in his textbook that listening is a learned behavior.*

3. *The local newscaster, Harvey Weise, predicts terrorism will continue in the United States.*

4. *Tom Watts, local T.V. meteorologist, predicts extended showers this afternoon.*

Unqualified or Qualified Statements

Statement sentences in the English language usually progress subject (noun)—verb (object); *Something is* or *Something does* (to something else). These are unqualified statements, grammatically in the indicative mood. They are concrete and objective in nature without the meaning or mood being modified. *Your answer is correct. You are great. He hit the guy with his fist.*

The qualified statements are in the subjunctive mood. These statements have words, phrases or clauses that make the basic statement conditional, exceptional, hypothetical and/or contingent on the verbal elements of the statement. Qualified statements are those that may include introductory or modifying words such as *reportedly, usually* and *allegedly. Perhaps your answer is correct. If conditions were different, you are great. Allegedly, he hit the guy with his fist.* Qualified statements include those with conditional verbs *appears* or *seems,* and hypothetical auxiliary verbs such as *could, should, would, may, might* and *must. Your answer could be correct. You might be great. It appears that he hit the guy with his fist.*

The critical listener should not accept the qualified statements as unqualified statements. One should realize that they are conditional and should be questioned. In relationship listening this is a difficult and sensitive task. Discuss how you each would respond to the following unqualified and qualified statements.

Usually, I am satisfied with your decisions.

I disagree with your attitude toward religion.

You appear to be upset with me.

I might go with you.

We are going to the celebration.

Critical Listening Qualified/Unqualified Statements Experience

One significant other reads/speaks the first four statements and discusses. After each read statement, the listener has the choice of labeling each statement as *qualified* or *unqualified*. Change the speaker/listener roles for the remaining four statements.

1. *Willis Carrier invented the air conditioner in 1906. (unqualified)*

2. *Perhaps, there may have been other air conditioners before the 1900's. (qualified)*

3. *If I were president and I may be someday, I would think about spreading the wealth. (qualified)*

4. *I think I overheard someone say he thought you may have won the election. (qualified)*

Switch speaker/listener roles.

1. *Today's fast food concept started in an A & W root beer stand in Sacramento, California in 1923. (unqualified)*

2. *The defendant could have been found guilty if the judge had permitted some of the prosecution's alleged evidence. (qualified)*

3. *Women, who were 21 years of age and citizens of the United States, were given the right to vote in 1920. (unqualified)*

4. *If an immigrant obtains a green card he could work in the United States. (qualified)*

Comparison

I.A. Richards contends that language is inherently the process of association and comparison. Every time the message uses the linking verb *be* (is, was, are, were) it is making a comparison of the subject with the predicate. For this purpose the critical listener must be careful about the two types of comparisons, literal and figurative.

The literal comparison is referred to as an analogy; whereas, the figurative comparison is referred to as a metaphor. A literal comparison is comparing the boxers Mohammed Ali with Joe Lewis, whereas, comparing Joe Lewis' *swing* with a *rusty gate* is a figurative comparison.

Figurative comparisons are creative, descriptive and interesting but not logical. It is like comparing apples with potatoes (a figurative analogy). The figurative comparison is found in clichés, idioms of informal prose and in simile and metaphors in poetry and rhetoric.

Remember that in Ogden and Richards' **Triangle of Meaning** on page 7 there is no direct relationship with the *word concept* and what it represents. Verbal meanings are in the minds of the beholder through association and comparison.

Critical Listener Comparison Experience

One significant other reads/speaks the first three items and the listener categorizes the statement as either a legitimate comparison or a figure of speech. Discuss after each statement. Switch roles for the second three statements.

1. *Sheila Bentley is another Barbara Walters.*

2. *John appears to be "death eating a cracker."*

3. *Effective listening is like sin; it is everywhere, but you have to search it out.*

Switch speaker/listener roles.

1. *Listening is like reading in that they both are receptive language skills.*

2. *Of the language skills, listening is the cream of the crop.*

3. *Political speaking is the tornado of the language skills, stirring up social controversy.*

Closing Process

The closing process, or the act of anticipation, is important in both comprehensive and critical listening. Interest and involvement in the message, whether it be motivated by wishing to understand or challenging what has been said, one needs to be aware of the closing process.

One can mentally process verbal concepts at a rate of approximately 400 words per minute, but the average speaking rate is 135 words per minute. The average speaking rate of a lecturer ranges from about 80 words per minute to 170 words per minute.

The listener must get involved through anticipation in order to maintain interest and prevent extraneous thoughts (daydreaming/mental preoccupation) from interfering. It is important that you get all of the information and not *second guess* the speaker. *How many of each species did Moses take on the ark?* Upon hearing that question, most people will reply 'two' and didn't listen that Moses didn't go on the ark. Try this one: *If I take two apples from three apples, how many do I have?* We often treat this as a math problem and answer 'one' when I actually took two.

The following illustrates the importance of closing, getting all the information and questioning. The grumpy, old, retired professor and his wife were traveling down the highway with a posted speed limit of 65-miles-an hour. The professor was driving 80-miles-per-hour when an officer of the law observed and clocked the car. The officer stopped the professor's car, went up to the driver's window and requested the professor's license. He then said, "*Sir, you were going 80-miles-an hour in a 65-mile-an-hour zone.*"

The professor blurted out, "*You must be wrong, I had the cruise control set at 65!*" His wife interjected, "*Honey, you know that you were going beyond the speed...*" The professor yelled at her, "*Shut your mouth and keep out of my business!*"

The officer wrote out a speeding ticket and said, "*I also noticed that you aren't wearing a seatbelt.*" The professor quickly countered, "*I was wearing my seatbelt but I took it off to get to my billfold containing my license.*"

The wife interjected, "*Honey you know you weren't wearing your seatbelt. You never wear you seatbelt.*"

The professor flings his arm back at her and says, *"Shut up! I told you to keep out of this."*

The officer writes out a seatbelt violation ticket and walks around to the passenger side window and says, *"Madam, does your husband always talk this mean to you?"* She quietly replied, *"Only when he is drunk."*

All the time you were reading this you were speculating what was going to come next and you were interested and attentive. Treat your conversations and lectures as a series of short stories or segments with which you can personally relate. Your attention span in comprehending what is being said is usually no longer than 15 to 20 minutes. If a person doesn't give you a break from intense concentration, then you should give yourself one by thinking about an extraneous subject for 30 seconds. After a short break you attend much better.

Critical Listening Closure Experience

In listening, we often *close* or assume our response before we listen to the speaker's complete statement or question. Read, listen and respond by writing down the reply to the requests. The first participant will read the first seven items while the second writes down the response, then exchange roles for the second seven items.

1. Can a man in Missouri marry his widow's sister?

2. How many birthdays does a man have in his average lifetime?

3. How many months have 28 days?

4. There has been a plane crash on the border between Canada and the U.S.A., there are six survivors. Where should they be buried?

5. If a farmer lost all but nine of his 17 sheep, how many would he have left?

6. How many outs are there in an inning of baseball?

7. Write the word V O T E on your paper.

Change speaker/listener roles.

1. You are the pilot of an airplane that is flying between KCI and Chicago. There are 150 passengers on board. The plane is halfway between the two cities. The carpeting in the plane is done in royal-blue and the seats are upholstered in a brilliant red. The hostesses have just finished serving lunch and everything has gone well thus far. The co-pilot's wife is three years younger than the pilot. How old is the pilot?

2. If there are 12 months and 52 weeks in the year, how many seconds are there?

3. If you had a dog and you tied her to a rope 15 feet long, how could she reach a bowl of dog food 50 feet away?

4. What was the tallest mountain in the world before Mount Everest was discovered?

5. If you had only one match and you entered a cold dark room that contained a kerosene lamp, an oil heater and wood-burning store, what would you light first?

6. Is it "nine and five make 13" or "nine and five are 13?"

7. A blind beggar had a brother. The blind beggar's brother died. However the brother who died had no brothers. How could that be?

Relationship/Empathetic Listening

Relationship listening involves discriminative and comprehensive listening and sometimes critical listening. However, the emphasis is on identifying with and sharing another's situation, feelings, emotions and/or motives.

Relationship listening has as its purpose to create mutual and reciprocal interest and caring. It most often is the purpose for listening with family and friends.

In a recent survey of Midwestern high school students and freshmen in college, the students reported that they listen most often to relate with someone. They reported that they spend more time listening to relate to friends than they do with parents, and their friends are their best listeners. They listen best to their friends because their friends listen best to them. They know that their friends are listening to them when they ask questions, ask for further information and *look at them*.

Empathetic Listening—Self Analysis Experience

Each significant other is to complete his/her self analysis and then share results on each item with his/her significant other.

1. For what purpose do you most frequently listen effectively to a significant other?
   (to comprehend information, to follow instructions, to relate, to analyze critically, to share feelings/emotions, to solve problems)

2. What is your most frequent topic of conversation with a significant other?
   (sports, sharing attitudes and feelings, art/recreation, other people/friends, local/world news, religion, money, social activities, your relationship, etc.)

3. What is the most ideal time for you to devote at least 15 minutes for empathetic communication with a significant other?
   (morning, noon, afternoon, evening, night)

4. In what physical context do you listen most effectively with a significant other?
   (riding in a car, at the kitchen table, in a living room/dining room, at an office desk, walking, working together)

5. What physical element affects your empathetic listening situation the most?
   (communicator axis, different eye levels, furniture/artifacts, area space, temperature, interfering noise, etc.)

6. *What assertive language factors influence you most in determining a speaker's attitudes toward you or the subject matter?*
   (use of first and second personal pronouns—direct address, active unqualified verbs, direct unqualified statements, use of analogies/metaphors, use of absolute quantifiers and modifiers)

7. *As an empathetic listener, what is your most effective verbal response to the speaker's concept-statements?*
   (closed questions, open-ended questions, paraphrasing, repeating what was just said and direct comments–"Good job," "right-on," and "oh boy")

8. *As an empathetic listener, what is your most effective non-verbal response to the speaker's concepts/statements?*
   (eye contact/referent, facial expressions, hand gesture/touch, body attitude, head nod or shake, vocal sounds–"hum" "ah" and "oh boy")

9. *What is most distracting when you are listening empathetically?*
   (allotted time, your mental preoccupation, inability to hear, interest in the topic, physical context/space/noise, speaker's attitude)

10. *Who is your most effective empathetic listener?*
    (friend, spouse, co-worker, sibling, an associate, pastor, teacher, etc.)

Empathetic/Non-Verbal Cues

In relationship listening, the emphasis is on interpretation of non-verbal cues. Research indicates that non-verbal elements make up 65 percent of the message's meaning in interpersonal or relationship communication. Of that, 38 percent of the message's meaning is conveyed by audible elements and 55 percent by visual elements. When any non-verbal behavior contradicts a verbal message, a listener will attend to the non-verbal elements.

Try it for yourself: Tell someone to listen and perform the following instructions. You say, *Raise your right arm* as you raise your right arm. *Raise your left arm* as you raise your left arm. *Raise your left arm* as you raise your right arm. More than likely, the listener would have raised his/her right arm. The non-verbal elements of audible, visual and contextual outweigh the words spoken.

Paralanguage

Paralanguage is the way something is said in regards to voice and speech. It is the characteristic style or manner of expressing yourself orally. This includes speech rate (including pauses and duration of words and phrases), pitch (heard as tone) inflection patterns, and intensity or loudness.

In relationship communication the average rate varies from 125-140 words per minute depending on the extent, purpose and topic of the message. A fast rate indicates a speaker's confidence and interest in what he/she is saying, whereas, a slow, deliberate rate with extended pauses and word durations indicates lack of confidence and interest in the message.

With the speaker using a deliberate or slow rate it is the responsibility of the listener to question the speaker's attitudes and involvement. Another method is to motivate the speaker through caring verbal responses and encouragement.

The speaker's use of the pause or intentional use of silence is an attempt to emphasize the verbal phrase that precedes the pause. The pause may also be used after a phrase to involve the listener in closing or finishing the phrase's meaning in the listener's own mind. The verbal pause *(ah, ahm, oh, etc.)* and the use of expletive phrases *(you know and now)* are usually used by the speaker as transitions and a request for the listener to indicate some response, but they often become habitual and create disfluency indicating that the speaker lacks confidence in him/herself and what he/she is saying.

The listener may compare the speaker's pauses with punctuation marks—short pauses as commas and longer pauses as sentence end punctuation. The difficulty arises with all the run-on sentences found in spoken style. Speech rate and rhythm consisting of word duration and pauses reflect the speaker's mood, emphasis and importance of the thought phrases. It also indicates the speaker's attitude toward him/herself, the message and the listener.

The speaker's pitch inflection patterns significantly indicate the speaker's attitudes toward the message and the listener. A listener's common complaint is that the speaker speaks in a monopitch and the listener hears a monotone. This gives the listener no indication of the speaker's feelings or attitudes toward the subject. Monotone speech is associated with a speaker who appears indifferent or lacks caring or overt involvement in the message. The listeners describe monopitch speakers as *impersonal* and *boring*.

A rising pitch at the end of a word or phrase indicates the speaker's uncertainty and incompleteness of thought. It can sometimes suggest humor. The lowered pitch at the end of a word or phrase indicates assertiveness, certainty and completeness of thought. When pitch rises and fall, this can indicate sarcasm, taunting or the speaker has hidden intentions.

The speaker's pitch inflection alters an *absolute word's* meaning. Absolute words such as *yes, no,* and *stop it* and conditional words such as *maybe* are changed in meaning by the inflection pattern. If you ask someone for some money and he/she says *no* while lowering his/her inflection, he/she means what was said, but if he/she uses a rising inflection *no*, you should pursue the request further for the speaker is not certain about his/her decision. If the speaker says, *nice shirt*, with a rising and falling pitch pattern, the listener should not take it as an intended compliment.

The speaker's pitch pattern and voice intensity or loudness indicate the speaker's interest and emotional involvement in what he/she is saying. You probably have heard someone in an argument say, *Don't raise your voice to me* or *Don't speak to me with that tone of voice*. Lack of voice intensity and variety indicate indifference and lack assertiveness, confidence and caring.

Arguments are excellent means of studying paralanguage as the elements are used in extremes. However, the elements used in arguments should also be evident in normal and common expressions only in a more reserved manner.

Visual Non-Verbals

An awareness and recognition of the speaker's use of the elements are important parts of relationship listening. This is as important as recognizing visual non-verbal elements.

The non-verbal listener's responses include both audible and visual elements. They represent the listener's interest, attitude and feeling. Audible non-verbal elements include: *Uhm* which is often used to show interest or to indirectly question what has been said. *Ah* is used as a sign of surprise or understanding. *Ahm* is used to get the speaker's attention and indicates that the listener wishes to interject a point. *Ah Hum* and *Uh Huh* signify agreement.

The visual listener's responses include: *mirroring* the facial expression and body attitude of the speaker in expressing empathy. Leaning forward signifies the listener is particularly interested or wants to hear the comments better. Leaning backward signifies that the listener is evaluating the speaker's comments. Crossing of the arms signifies defensiveness or a judgmental attitude. Front nodding of the head indicates approval. Shaking the head sideways indicates disagreement or misunderstanding. Shrugging of the shoulders often indicates indifference or *don't know*. Extending the hands with palms up indicate a need to touch. Gesturing with a circle of the thumb and index finger signifies *ok* or approval. The thumbs-up hand gesture indicates approval or *good job*.

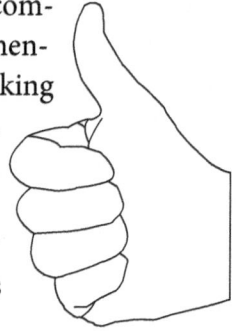

As with all non-verbal cues, it is important to consider all available contextual cues and the people interacting in deciphering specific meanings. Often significant others develop their own code of audible and visual non-verbal responses. Whatever the code developed, such cues can be used with verbal expressions of support and encouragement.

Non-Verbal Response Analysis (discuss results)

1. *How does your significant other respond non-verbally when he/she questions what you are saying?*
   (eye movement, forehead/eyebrows, lips, body attitude/movement, hand gestures, vocal sounds)

2. *How do you respond non-verbally when you question what your significant other is saying?*

3. *How does your significant other respond non-verbally when he/she disagrees with what you are saying?*

4. *How do you respond non-verbally when you disagree with what your significant other is saying?*

5. *How does your significant other respond non-verbally when he/she is really interested in what you have to say?*

6. *How do you respond non-verbally when you are really interested in what your significant other is saying?*

7. *How do your respond non-verbally when you are having difficulty in understanding what your significant other is saying?*

8. *How does your significant other respond when he/she is having difficulty understanding what you are saying?*

9. *What non-verbal cues do your display indicating that you are happy or sad?*

10. *What non-verbal cues does your spouse display indicating that he/she is happy or sad?*

11. *What do you believe is the strongest non-verbal indicator of your significant other's attitude or feelings in a conversation with you?*

12. *How important is hand touching in your relationship communication?*

13. *What is the most distracting factor in your communication with your significant other?*
    (your own characteristics, your significant other, the situation, topic interest, time, etc.)

In relationship listening, the listener needs to be aware of the speaker's intent and attitude as reflected by both his/her verbal and non-verbal cues. The speaker may indicate assertiveness, uncertainty, indifference or conciliatory intent.

Recognizing Speaker's Intent Experience

One significant other who is serving as the speaker, chooses to be assertive, or uncertain or indifferent or conciliating while expressing the first five statements below. The speaker is to match the audible and visual cues he/she believes would accompany each statement provided. The listener is to attempt to recognize the intended meaning of the each statement after the statement is made. Listener notes whether the intended statement is assertive, uncertain, indifferent or conciliatory. Change roles for the second five statements.

1. *Frankly, I couldn't care less about your opinion!*

2. *I don't know and I'm not sure I care to know.*

3. *I've respected you for a long time, but I can't accept your opinion on this matter.*

4. *You are wrong.*

5. *Knowing you, I'm sure it's a good idea.*

Change speaker/listener roles.

1. *I appreciate your interest and comments.*

2. *It sounds as if you are certain about your opinion.*

3. *It sounds as if you have really thought this out.*

4. *I agree with what you say but I can't accept it coming from you.*

5. *I can't believe anything you say.*

Recognizing Speaker's Mood/Attitude Experience

One significant other will say each of the first five statements using his/her voice as an indicator of one of the specific moods: 1) questioning, 2) assertive, 3) sarcastic, and 4) indifferent. Significant others change roles for second five statements. Check and discuss the listener's response after each statement.

1. *Who did this?*

2. *No.*

3. *Good job.*

4. *You are beautiful (handsome).*

5. *Well done.*

Change speaker/listener roles.

1. *Nice hat.*

2. *Meet me later.*

3. *OK.*

4. *Why?*

5. *Who?*

Visual Non-Verbal Cues in Empathetic Listening

In relationship listening, recognizing visual non-verbal elements of the messages is extremely important. That is why person-to-person communication is much more effective than telephone, video and/or electronic media. Without the visual inter-action, the messages are more abstract. They require much more interpretation of meanings, speaker's intent, emotional involvement and attitudes toward the listener, the subject and him/herself in regards to the topic. Visual non-verbal elements are the 1) eyes, 2) forehead and eyebrows, 3) lips/mouth, 4) hand gestures/touch, and 5) body attitude.

Eye contact and movement are the most important visual elements in recognizing the speaker's believability, emotional involvement, attitudes and interest in what is being communicated. Eye contact and reference are reciprocal between the speaker and the listener. You perhaps have said to someone, *Look at me when you are talking to me.*

The eyes are the windows of the mind through which the listener can determine how the speaker is internalizing what he/she is saying. Supposedly, if the speaker is visually processing what he/she is saying, their eyes will move up to the left. If the speaker is aurally processing what is being said through hearing, the eyes glance down to the right. Without eye contact or reference, the speaker is not really thinking about what he/she is saying and is demonstrating little if any involvement in what is being said.

When one wears dark glasses, he/she is depriving the listener of essential information. *Shades* may appear cool, but not for one with whom you may wish to establish a significant relationship.

The forehead and eyebrows mirror the speaker's emotions as well as his/her thought involvement in the message. The lines on the forehead indicate concentration and lack of forehead lines suggest lack of interest in either the message or the listener. The speaker who wears a cap pulled down to the eyebrows denies the listener important cues as to the speaker's attitude and feelings. Lip and mouth movements suggest the assertiveness and confidence in that which he/she is saying. Those who are not confident in what they are saying, tend not to move their lips in articulating the message.

Gesturing within a three-foot distance between speaker and listener indicates the speaker's involvement in what he/she is saying. If the speaker's gestures are broad or call the listener's attention away from the message, they are of little value to either the speaker or the listener. (The more relevant body movements on the part of either the speaker or the listeners, or the more dynamic the speaker is, the more believable and involved the speaker and listener are.) At closer distance between communicators, a light social touch on the arm, shoulder or hand expresses empathy on the part of both the speaker and the listener in relationship listening.

Being aware of the speaker's visual non-verbal messages and their importance in relationship communication is of utmost importance. Together analyze and discuss the following visual cues quiz.

Put the corresponding expression's letter on the blank next to the emotion.

___ 1. Indifference	___ 7. Embarrassment	___ 12. Pride
___ 2. Anger	___ 8. Frustration	___ 13. Fear
___ 3. Confusion	___ 9. Love	___ 14. Contentment
___ 4. Excitement	___ 10. Worry	___ 15. Satisfaction
___ 5. Happiness	___ 11. Distrust	___ 16. Sadness
___ 6. Determination		

1. I, 2. F, 3. E, 4. J, 5. B, 6. C, 7.A, 8. K, 9. N, 10. L, 11. D, 12. G, 13. M, 14. P, 15. O, 16. H

The Physical Context and Time Influence on Listening Effectiveness

The non-verbal elements of the surrounding area significantly influence effective communication. These non-verbal elements include: 1) time, 2) levels, 3) axis and 4) space.

Time Considerations

Time considerations include biological time, promptness and duration. The communicators need to choose quality time when neither communicator is exhausted nor preoccupied with upcoming scheduled events. Biological time preferences vary with individuals, but one should be aware of his/her significant other's time preference as well as his/her own.

When do you communicate best—morning, noon, afternoon, evening, night? Empathetic communication involves physical, emotional and mental attention of both participants. I have taught a class at 7:00 a.m., and believe me, most young people do not listen well at that time of day. They were resentful that I was wide awake.

Spoken communication is also hindered when one or both are preoccupied with an allotted time frame. Saying to the other communicator, *I have precisely 10 minutes for this conversation!* destroys empathetic communication. *Being on time* for the session demonstrates respect and appropriate consideration of the other communicator. *Being late* is a definite insult to the other communicator and it certainly interferes with the development of interpersonal trust. Tardiness is often associated with one who has an indifferent attitude in regards to either the other communicator or the message. Effective empathetic listening occurs between 15 and 30 minutes duration after which effectiveness diminishes. It takes three to four minutes of pleasantries at the beginning of the conversation before effective listening begins.

Levels

Eye level plays a significant role in effective communication. Both communicators should be at approximately the same eye level. The seated position lends itself to better eye contact and referent or better association.

Axis

The angle at which the communicators are positioned is one of the behaviors that can best predict the relationship's success. This is where axis comes in. Axis refers to the symmetry or configuration of the two communicators to each other. Axis

is best illustrated by visualizing each communicator as a number on a clock and the physical relationship to each other by the hands.

The most advantageous axis for communication would be with one communicator at 12 and the second at either 3 or 9. This axis is best because it provides the opportunity for eye contact and eye referent without constant awareness.

PREFERRED   CHALLENGING

3 or 9,   12 direct
4 and 7 also acceptable

Space/Proximity/Furniture

Space between the communicators affects the effectiveness of listening. Effective listening diminishes as the communicators increase the distance from two to five feet between them. However, intrusion into the other person's personal space (18 inches) also affects the effectiveness of the verbal message. At this close proximity, the spoken words become far less important than does the physical behavior and its intimidating factors.

Examples of Space/Proximity/Furniture, Levels and Axis

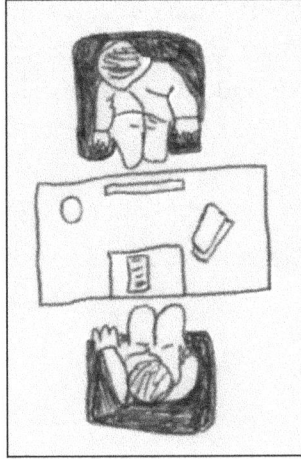

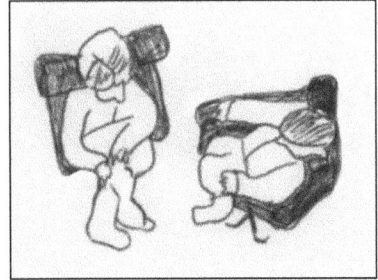

Role of Responding Verbally

The effective listener responds both verbally and non-verbally to the significant other's spoken expression. Verbal responses include questioning, paraphrasing and verbatim repeating what the speaker says. An involved listener will ask questions for clarification and more specific information. Lack of questioning indicates lack of attention or indifference on the part of the listener.

Asking questions enhances the listener's responsibility in understanding and appreciating what the speaker means. Questions regulate the exchange of speaker/listener roles in the conversation and prevent extended monologue. Questions aid the speaker to better understand his/her expression and should be specific and concrete in nature. Paraphrasing is an attempt to abbreviate, abstract and exemplify the speaker's concept by presenting it in the listener's words from his/her perspective. *If I understand you correctly* . . . provides the necessary dialog for communication. For the listener to repeat verbatim a short phrase enables the speaker to hear his/her own words from a different perspective. Repeating verbatim requires the listener to listen carefully. It provides an opportunity to change conversation roles and prevents an over-extended monologue.

Responding to a Series of Actual Personal Statements Experience

One significant other speaks a set of statements using actual (truthful) description of his/her feelings to fill in the blanks indicated. After the speaker completes the series, the listener will respond by asking the speaker three questions or paraphrasing or mirroring (repeating what the speaker said.) After the speaker completes the four items, the speaker exchanges roles with the listener.

1. *I think the thing that you do in our relationship that pleases me most is...... When you...... I feel...... I hope you will......*

2. *I think the thing that you do in our relationship that irritates me most is...... When you...... I feel...... I wish that......*

3. *I think in our conversations the topic that makes me most uncomfortable is...... When we try to talk about...... I feel...... and I wish we......*

4. *I think that your strongest communication skill is...... When you...... I feel...... I hope......*

Conclusion

Now that you both have completed your study, you should better understand the language skill of listening, your own listening behavior and preferences, and the listening behavior and preferences of your significant other. I hope you have learned how to better listen and communicate with someone you care about through this method of teaching. Please share the following poem with each other.

Thanks a Million for Listening
By Bob Bohlken

Thank you for listening to me so very well!
You are truly kind and empathetic, I can tell.
Your purpose for listening to me is unselfish and clear,
As we attempt together to alleviate my concerns and fear.
You attend with your ears and eyes every word I say and expressions I show,
My thoughts, my analyses, my feelings, you appear to understand and know,
Creating a kinship of our minds that continues to grow.

You appear to interpret, relate and respond to what I say and do,
As if our sharing and caring for each other is through and through.
You respond in a gentle, considerate reflective way,
As a true friend listens purposefully to what I have to say.
It's as if you know listening is caring and reciprocal.
It's a dynamic relationship based on strength, character and love above all.
Your listening to me is especially nice,
Like with God, there is no interpretation for unwanted advice.
Thanks for listening to me as well as you do,
I hope I am as good of a listener for you.

ABOUT THE AUTHOR

Bob Bohlken, Ph. D., Communication Professor Emeritus, retired from Northwest Missouri State University, Maryville, Missouri, in 2000 after a 30 year tenure. His academic areas of expertise include *Listening, Semantics, Interpersonal Communication/Non-Verbal,* and *Communicative Credibility and Trust.*

He holds a B.S. in Language Arts Education with Distinction, Nebraska State College, Peru; Master of Arts Degree in Communication (Thesis: **Comparison of Written and Spoken Narrative Language Styles**) University of Nebraska, Lincoln; Doctorate of Philosophy in Communication (Dissertation: **A Descriptive Study of the Relationship Between the Communication Variable of Interpersonal Trust and Speech Teacher Effectiveness at the College Level**) University of Kansas, Lawrence.

Dr. Bohlken is a Korean War and Cold War army veteran (1953-1956). He has been a member of the American Legion for 60 years and is a member of the Veterans of Foreign Wars. He is a life member of the International Listening Association and was inducted into the Hall of Fame in 2006. He is also a member of the International Society for General Semantics, Missouri Folklore Society, and the National Communication Society. Dr. Bohlken is a life member of the International Optimist Club of Maryville, the Nodaway County Historical Society and the St. Gregory Catholic Church. He is actively involved in numerous community service efforts and serves on the Nodaway County Senior Center Senate.

Dr. Bohlken and his wife Mary Riley Bohlken have been married for 55 years and are the proud parents of two children—Katy Gumm and Dan Bohlken and four grandchildren—Bobby and Brandon Gumm and Faith and Alex Bohlken.

He writes a human interest column for the weekly *Nodaway News Leader* and is the author of two children's books and five leisure reading, human interest books. He has written numerous articles for academic journals, presented at numerous academic conferences and continues to present communication workshops and lectures to civic organizations and schools.

ORDER FORM

Here's how to get your own copy of books by Bob Bohlken, Ph.D.

		QUANTITY	$ TOTAL

**Learning to Listen with
Significant Others** $14.95 _____ _____

**Listening to the Mukies and Their
Character Building Activities** $14.95 _____ _____

**Listening to Rural Midwestern
Idioms/Folk Sayings** $9.95 _____ _____

Shipping:

Up to $50............................$6.50

$51-$199............................$8.75

$200 or more.........$12.00-$20.00

Subtotal $_____

Shipping/Handling $_____

7.975% Missouri Tax $_____

Total Enclosed $_____

Payment Enclosed $_____ ❑ Check_____ ❑ Credit Card _____

Card Number _____ Expiration Date_____

Signature_____

Make check or money order payable to:
Images Unlimited, P.O. Box 305, Maryville, MO 64468

Name _____

Street _____

City _____ State _____ Zip _____